BILL PEET
An Autobiography

Houghton Mifflin Company
Boston 1989

To the girl I met in art school

By Bill Peet

The Ant and the Elephant
Big Bad Bruce
Bill Peet An Autobiography
Buford the Little Bighorn
The Caboose Who Got Loose
Capyboppy
Chester the Worldly Pig
Cowardly Clyde
Cyrus the Unsinkable Sea Serpent
Eli
Ella
Encore for Eleanor
Farewell to Shady Glade
Fly, Homer, Fly
The Gnats of Knotty Pine
How Droofus the Dragon Lost His F
Hubert's Hair-Raising Adventure

Huge Harold
Jennifer and Josephine
Jethro and Joel Were a Troll
Kermit the Hermit
The Kweeks of Kookatumdee
The Luckiest One of All
Merle the High Flying Squirrel
No Such Things
Pamela Camel
The Pinkish, Purplish, Bluish Egg
Randy's Dandy Lions
Smokey
The Spooky Tail of Prewitt Peacock
The Whingdingdilly
The Wump World
Zella, Zack and Zodiac

Library of Congress Cataloging-in-Publication Data

Peet, Bill.
  Bill Peet : an autobiography / Bill Peet.
    p. cm.
    Summary: The well-known author and illustrator relates the story of his life and work.
  ISBN 0-395-50932-7
  1. Peet, Bill—Biography. 2. Authors, American—20th century—Biography. 3. Children's stories—Authorship. 4. Illustrators—United States—Biography. 5. Animators—United States—Biography. 6. Walt Disney Productions. [1. Peet, Bill. 2. Authors, American. 3. Illustrators.] I. Title.
PS3566.E29Z464 1989
813'.54—dc19
[B]
[92]   88-37067
                                 CIP
                                  AC

In that compartment of the brain where visual memories are stored mine has been cluttered with an endless assortment of things starting with the two pigs we raised in my birthplace of Grandview, Indiana.

And yet I can't remember my father and mother or my two brothers in Grandview. That was during the First World War, and my father was drafted into the army before I was three.

1

My mother was a graduate of a teacher's college, and when she found a teaching job in Indianapolis my widow grandmother, my two brothers, and I left Grandview to join her in the big city. My first memory of Indianapolis was a view from the front window of the house we rented. Beyond a vacant lot was a railroad, and moving along under a gloomy gray sky I saw a long train of flat cars loaded with snow-covered army tanks.

2

My father's regiment was never shipped over to France, and when the war ended in 1918 he was still in training camp in Kentucky.

But when he left the army he never came to join us in Indianapolis as Mother had expected.

Whenever anyone asked about him she always explained, "He's a traveling salesman out on the road somewhere."

My brothers and I had never known our father, so his absence had very little effect on us except for the times when other kids would taunt us about not having a daddy.

With Grandmother running the household and taking care of everyone's needs, our family seemed quite complete. And life was even better when Grandmother used her life's savings to buy a house near the east end of the city, just a ten-minute trot from the open countryside.

4

That house on North Riley Avenue was where I spent the happiest years of my boyhood.

My favorite room in the house was the attic, where I enjoyed filling fat five-cent tablets with a hodgepodge of drawings. Drawing became my number one hobby as soon as I could manipulate a crayon or pencil well enough to put my favorite things on paper.

I have no idea how well I drew then since all those early drawings are long gone. However, I must have drawn fairly well or I couldn't have enjoyed it so much.

The drawings on these pages were done during the planning of this book with no attempt to re-create my boyhood drawings from memory.

I drew for hours at a time just for the fun of it, and yet I was hoping to find some practical reason to draw for the rest of my life. But when I entered grade school, my drawing habit suddenly became a problem.

There was an art class once a week but that wasn't nearly enough, and no fun at all. The art teacher decided what we were to draw, and they were never my kind of things.

So I drew on the sly in all my other classes by hiding a tablet in my desk and sneaking a drawing into it now and then. Very often I'd get caught at it and the teacher would snatch my tablet away and warn me to stick to my studies.

I also drew in my books, on the margins of the pages, which was graphic evidence that I had spent very little time reading the text.

But when it came time for the used book sales my illustrated books were best sellers. The kids loved my drawings and I suppose those books could be considered the very first ones I ever illustrated for children.

7

Drawing was the perfect indoor hobby during the cold, windy Indiana winters, but in the summer the stifling hot attic was no place to be.

It was time for the great outdoors, and with my brothers and the neighborhood boys I was off into the countryside wading along the creeks that ran through shady ravines.

Our safaris must have resembled a Halloween procession, since each of us wore a different outfit and his favorite hat.

8

Mine was a World War helmet, a "tin hat" I bought for two bits at an army surplus store along with a bullet belt that was all pockets.

We were after small game such as turtles, frogs, tadpoles, minnows, and crayfish—a "bring 'em back alive" safari with no intentions of killing anything. Nevertheless, very few of those tiny creatures we captured lasted more than a week in our wash-tub aquariums.

Most of the tadpoles survived to complete their miraculous transformation as day by day their tails diminished simultaneously with the growth of their legs.

Once their metamorphosis was complete, we returned the tiny frogs to the creek, all except the ones that escaped and went hopping off into the neighborhood.

Watching tadpoles turn into frogs was fun for a while, but I was much more interested in catching one of the larger frogs so I could put him in a glass jar and make drawings of him.

They were much too alert to be taken by surprise, and if you came within ten feet of one he slipped away into the shadowy depths of the creek.

I do remember catching one full-grown frog, and I remember it well because of a snake. The frog was swimming near the surface of the creek unaware that I was only a few feet away.

In one quick grab I had him by a hind leg. Then, at the same instant, a snake shot out of a hole in the bank and seized the frog by the head.

Suddenly we were having a frantic tug of war with the frog caught in the middle.

12

It was touch and go until I finally jerked the frog free. Then in a flash the snake was back in his hole.

I thought sure I had saved the frog from certain death until I plopped him back into the water and he went drifting downstream limp and lifeless.

The snake was a deadly poisonous water moccasin, and his fangs had punctured the poor frog. All I had done was cheat the snake out of his lunch.

It has always been difficult for me to accept nature's cruel ways of keeping a balance among the animals — all the savagery and the suffering, with so many being sacrificed for others to survive.

14

Yet nature's merciless ways were never more cruel than the slow, silent death caused by poisonous waste spilling from pipes down into the creek, spreading a brownish purple scum over the water, where dead fish floated belly up and a nauseating stench filled the air.

But I prefer to remember the life and beauty of the creek, the brilliant blue dragonflies darting among the cattails, the lazy mud turtles sunning themselves on warm rocks, schools of minnows flashing in and out of the sunlight, and the water striders gliding lightly over the glassy surface in the shade of the willows and sycamores.

My favorite spot in the creek was deep enough for swimming and also conveniently near a railroad bridge where steam loco-

motives came thundering overhead just often enough to keep a devoted train watcher happy.

To me those giant engines were by far the greatest things on wheels, marvelous huffing, puffing, steaming works of art.

The best place to get acquainted with the great locomotives was at the Union Station, near downtown Indianapolis. The trains were on the upper level of the station, and only people with tickets and those who were there to see them off were allowed up the stairs to the tracks.

So I joined many good-bye parties going up those stairs, and while the people were crowding aboard the coaches I was feasting my eyes on the complex anatomy of the great iron horse up front.

I was determined to memorize every detail so I could put it all into the locomotive drawings I planned to make in the future, and there would be hundreds.

19

Since I was so very fond of trains, it was a special treat to go on my first train trip with my brothers to my grandfather's farm in southern Indiana.

Our old two-car train took its own sweet time clickety-clacking along through a rolling landscape of fields, barns, and pastures dotted with horses, cows, and pigs.

Past small towns, over rivers and creeks, and through forests.
I loved the farm country, so it was a luxury to view miles and
miles of it from the coach window. A fine show to the very last
scene, which was the railway station in the historic old town of
Vincennes.

There we were met by our grandfather in his dusty old touring car and we were off again, bouncing along for the last thirty-five miles on rambling dirt roads that were forever doubling back and forth all over the county.

Grandfather was gruff and didn't seem at all happy to meet us, and since he had nothing to say we went jolting and bumping along in silence. As we passed through a dense woods he finally muttered, "They found a dead man back in those trees years ago," and that was all.

The next voice we heard was the raucous barking of the frowsy big farm dog, Towser, as we pulled up by the gate to the front yard of the farm house.

Grandfather's house was a dreary old mansion in need of paint, and the lawn grew knee high as if the place were deserted. The gloomy appearance of the house reflected the sad state of the farm, the years of crop failures and poor investments.

With most of the rooms closed off, the house was ghostly and cheerless. Grandfather, Grandmother, and our two middle-aged aunts occupied only a part of the ground floor.

Life abounded in the huge gray barn, which was a hostelry for hundreds and open to all comers. In the stables and pens were horses, mules, cattle, and pigs. There were cats and kittens all over the place. Owls and pigeons roosted high on the rafters above the hayloft, and under the corn crib and the feed bins scampered rats and mice by the dozens. Now and then weasels, skunks, and snakes came visiting in the night.

If we expected an adventurous, footloose summer, Grandfather had other ideas.

Early the next morning, after breakfast, he put us to work sawing up great piles of dead fruit trees into firewood. Then we mowed the spacious, overgrown front lawn, weeded the vegetable garden, picked apples and cherries, and did whatever Grandfather could think of to keep us busy.

On the farm there was no time for play or tomfoolery. Aunt Minnie and Aunt Martha were out in the barn before daybreak milking the cows.

Then they scurried back to the kitchen to join Grandmother in baking bread and pies, canning fruit, churning butter, making cottage cheese, putting up jam and jelly, washing and ironing, and scrubbing the floors.

Grandfather spent the morning chewing tobacco on the back porch. Then, after lunch, he retired to the parlor for a nap in his big leather easy chair.

Once we discovered Grandfather's habit of dozing off after lunch we were finally footloose, at least for a few hours.

Towser had been waiting for us to spring into action, and as we went tearing across the fields and pastures he kept circling ahead of us barking ecstatically.

We headed straight for the dark, dense woods beyond the fields, hoping to catch sight of a bear or a wolf or some large wild animal, even though Aunt Martha explained that no bears or wolves had been seen around there since she was a child.

Even if there had been any bears or wolves left over, Towser's incessant high-pitched barking would have sent them into hiding, and there'd be no chance whatever of seeing one.

The only wildlife to be seen were some feisty squirrels scolding Towser from the treetops and the ever present cottontails bounding through the bush.

But we did happen onto a remarkable swimming hole created by an underground spring welling up into an abandoned stone quarry. It was a great discovery, and we returned for an icy cold swim many times during that steaming hot summer.

Grumpy Grandfather couldn't possibly spoil my memories of that marvelous old farm. I remember what great fun we had in the hayloft of that huge barn, swinging on ropes, leaping off crossbeams and rafters into mountains of hay. The only hazard was the chance of landing on a hen's egg laid in the hay much too long ago.

31

When I think of the young spring calves I have to laugh. They were always ready to play, and we dropped down on all fours to butt heads with them. But we were no match for their rock-hard skulls, and they got the best of it. The only way we could win was to cheat and jerk a leg out from under them.

It was hard to imagine those sprightly youngsters growing up to resemble their father, a big, dull-witted brute of a bull, or to be anything like their mothers, the sullen, cantankerous cows.

32

After we left the farm old Towser was very much in my thoughts. I wondered if our visit was the only fun the poor dog ever had. Towser deserved a better fate than to be stuck for the rest of his days with a family of old people. That rambunctious Huck Finn of a dog deserved companions of his own kind to go chasing around with, and have a few laughs.

I believe some dogs *do* laugh, in a panting sort of way. I'm sure old Towser did. And there was no doubt of his broad grin.

Animal personalities have always intrigued me, and the desire to find out more about them made a reader out of me.

Our neighborhood library was an old frame mansion crammed full of books, and even though it was about four miles away I was a regular customer in the worst winter weather.

Most of the books with first-hand information about wild animals were written by big game hunters—large, thick volumes that were difficult to read.

34

Their hunting experiences were usually exaggerated to dramatize the danger to themselves while making the animals appear as ferocious and menacing as possible. The photos were mostly of dead animals, lifeless hulks, with members of the hunting party posed triumphantly beside them.

My favorite animal stories were by Ernest Thompson Seton, a naturalist who illustrated his own books. His realistic stories, with their sad endings, nearly brought me to tears, and yet I read them again and again. His excellent black-and-white illustrations were drawn from animals in the wild, which was what I hoped to do someday.

I often dreamed of going to Africa and sketching my favorite animals on the spot, which seemed far too ambitious for an eleven-year-old until an ad in a boy's magazine caught my eye:

TAXIDERMIST WANTED FOR AFRICAN SAFARI.

Then, by remarkable coincidence, on the very next page was another ad:

LEARN THE ART OF TAXIDERMY — MAKE BIG MONEY.

And there was no age limit mentioned in either ad.

I immediately filled out the coupon, requesting an information pamphlet from the Northwestern School of Taxidermy, in Omaha, Nebraska.

36

If I should ever go on the safari, I realized the shooting of the animals would horrify me. But I would have nothing to do with that part of it or even have to watch.

My plan was to find time between jobs and go wandering out on the veldt and sketch as many animals as possible.

However, when I received a contract from the taxidermy school calling for two hundred dollars to be paid in so many installments, *POOF!* went my dream of going to Africa.

Two hundred dollars was a mountain of money, a staggering amount for someone who made money a penny at a time by selling newspapers.

Back in the twenties a penny was not to be sneezed at, and a nickel was a highly respectable coin. A nickel was the price of a chocolate bar, a hot dog, a sack of peanuts, an ice cream cone, a box of Cracker Jack with a prize in it, a root beer, or a Coke, and for me the best of all nickel bargains was a box of crayons.

During my years of peddling newspapers the biggest headline I ever shouted was "LINDBERGH FLIES THE ATLANTIC! Extra! Extra! Read all about it!"

The best day of the year for newsboys was Memorial Day, the day of the Indianapolis 500. We were trucked out to the speedway at five in the morning to get ahead of the crowds, then dropped off in the weedy infield with bundles of papers.

Long before race time the infield was jammed with parked cars and customers, and we were selling our special editions with the race line-ups as fast as we could make change.

As the race got under way the bootleg whiskey and the hot sun took effect, putting our customers in a festive holiday "keep the change" mood, which multiplied our profits into more than we made the rest of the year — a real bonanza!

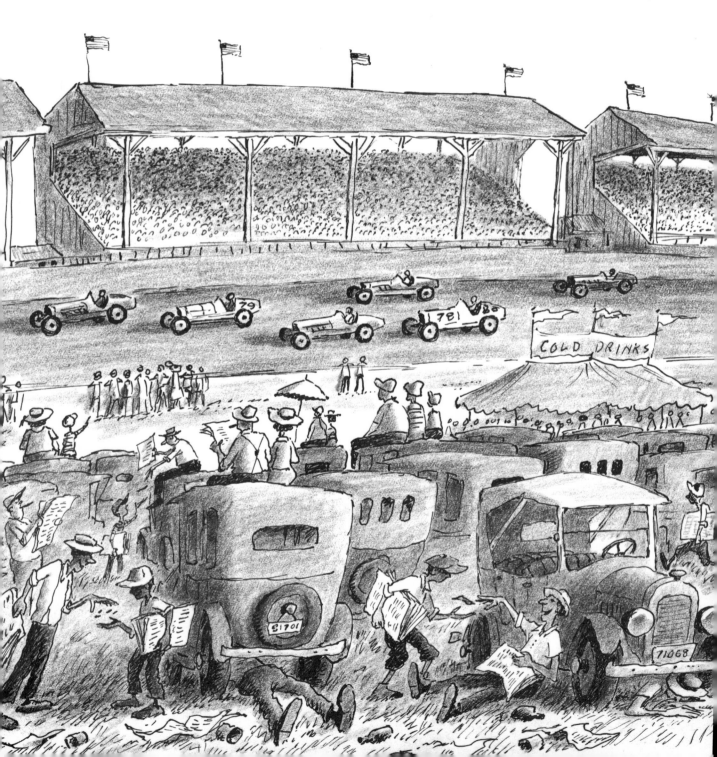

For a few days after the race I drew dozens of race cars in action, some of the crackups I'd seen—wheels flying off, cars hurtling over the wall, and some exploding into flames. Yet I was never a racing fan and never cared who won the 500.

My favorite sport was always football. I loved to play the game in vacant lots with the neighborhood kids.

The players varied in age and size to such ridiculous extremes
that it was like a skirmish between rabbits, rhinos, goats, and
hippos, and I was usually one of the skinniest of the rabbits.

But I was quick on my feet, and time after time I sidestepped

42

and zigzagged my way past all the tacklers and a couple of trees to score touchdowns.

At age eleven I was serious about becoming a football star and I would have gladly traded my drawing ability for a few pounds of muscle.

In desperation I sent for the Charles Atlas course in muscle building, and within a week I received a pamphlet full of photos of muscle men including before and after photos to prove what miraculous results the skinniest men could expect.

Then there was the price of the muscles, which was just as far out of reach as the price of the taxidermy course had been.

Without the money to build a new body, they still called me Skinny when I graduated from grade school.

I suspect that some of those teachers gave me passing grades just to make sure I moved on and took my sneaky drawing habit with me. Whatever the case, I was happy to have made my escape to enjoy a carefree summer before entering high school in the fall.

But the summer of 1928 was anything but carefree. It turned out to be a disastrous time.

44

One afternoon my father suddenly appeared, driving up to our house in a rickety model T Ford.

I recall it vividly since I was the only one home, and it also marked the end of a happy childhood.

After ten years on the road as a salesman he was travel weary and flat broke, and out of desperation he decided to join us.

Grandmother would have nothing to do with him, and as soon as she finished her housework and prepared the meals she retreated to her small bedroom upstairs. She could see trouble ahead and wanted no part of it.

Sure enough, in a very short time my parents *were* having their troubles.

My father demanded money to finance another sales trip, and when my mother refused fierce quarreling broke out.

Their loud shouting matches went on for days and sometimes far into the night. I stood up to my father one night calling him a big bully, and *POWIE!* I caught a fist in the head that sent me sprawling.

There was no stopping the war until Mother gave in and paid him off. Then my father was on his way again, out on the road peddling everything from house paint to popcorn machines.

In a week or two he would be back flat broke again and in need of more money, and the quarreling would start all over.

Grandmother kept her distance during those stormy times, and even when my father was gone she refused to be part of the family. All the unhappiness was more than she could bear, and one afternoon when all of us were home, Grandmother suddenly called out from her bedroom, a loud, mournful wail that echoed all through the house.

In a panic we rushed upstairs to the foot of her bed just as she made one last desperate gasp for breath, then died of a heart attack.

My mother, my brothers, and I were devastated. It was hard to believe that my grandmother was gone, and so suddenly.

That horrifying moment of watching her die haunted me for many years.

Soon after Grandmother's death her house was sold so the money could be divided among the heirs.

Moving out of 518 North Riley Avenue was a painful uprooting, and after that we would be renting and moving many times, and we would always be strangers in the neighborhood.

It was a miserable time to be starting Tech High School, which was one of the biggest high schools in the country.

Entering the campus was like being lost in a foreign city without a familiar face in sight.

But then many of my grade school classmates couldn't afford
to go on to high school in those hard times — they had to go out
and find a job. I shouldn't have been going to high school either,
since my only concern was getting it over with in four years.

48

Life had become much too serious to be dreaming about an art career, so I didn't enroll in any art classes.

I signed up for algebra, English, civics, history, Latin, and physical education. It was a heavy schedule for someone who barely made it through grade school.

After my last class I often put off going home and hung around the football field to watch the Tech teams practice. There were no quick-footed scampering jack rabbits out there, even on the freshman teams. They were all rhinos and hippos practicing bruising, line-plunging power football, and every few minutes an injured player hobbled off to the sidelines.

I was a fairly tall ninety-pounder, a perfect "before" for a Charles Atlas ad, and yet I still wished I could get out there in the thick of the action.

In June, at the end of the school year, I had failed in every
one of my classes but physical education. No one failed in physical
ed as long as he could do a couple of chin-ups. But that class
was worth only half a credit, and one credit for a whole year. At
that rate I'd be stuck in high school for thirty-two years.

That was 1929, the year of the stock market crash, when rich
men who lost fortunes leaped off the tops of tall buildings.

51

We were into the Great Depression, and unemployed men took
to the road like hobos on the way to just anywhere hoping to
find work.

I remember seeing hundreds of them riding on boxcars, some
going east, others going west to wherever the train might take
them.

We had our own unique brand of poverty. While my mother
made a fairly good income teaching handwriting, my father continued to come and go as a traveling salesman, squandering so
much money he kept us poor.

In those dreary times my brothers and I became a quarrelsome
threesome, no doubt soured by the unhappy home atmosphere,
and we seldom went anywhere together.

Once in a while I walked across town to one of our old neighborhoods, hoping to find someone I knew.

One day I ran into a boy who had been in my class in grade school, and he asked how I liked Tech.

When I told him about flunking all my classes but physical education he was surprised that I hadn't taken any art classes.

"I got some credits in art," he said, "and I can hardly draw at all. But you're *really* good. Art would be a breeze for you."

The following fall I dropped a couple of my academic courses and added some art classes—fine art and commercial art. In both classes the art teachers were immediately impressed, not only with my drawing, but also with my painting and sculpture.

As my grade school classmate predicted, the art classes *were* a breeze, and they also gave me a head of steam that carried over into my other classes.

In the next four years I earned my thirty-two credits and even absorbed a smattering of math and English along the way.

Another triumph was getting one of my sketches in the 1933 school yearbook along with photos of the football team.

It was a pen drawing of a football pileup just above the picture of the Tech varsity.

Then to top it all off I was awarded a scholarship to the John Herron Art Institute in Indianapolis. My dream of making art a career suddenly seemed much more realistic.

Art school was a wonderful new beginning in more ways than one.

In my very first class, on the elements of design, I found myself staring at a girl in the front row.

In a few weeks I learned that she was Margaret Brunst, from the small town of Ladoga, about forty miles west of Indianapolis.

Attractive girls always unnerved me, so it must have taken quite a few more weeks for me to manage so much as an awkward hello to her.

Now Margaret and I have been married fifty years as of last November.

Even though problems at home continued to disturb me, those years at art school were some of the happiest of my life.

Not only did I find Margaret there, I received a great deal of valuable instruction in drawing, painting, and design. It was all peaches and cream, with no devilish academic problems to boggle my mind.

However, I did have a problem with one instructor who was annoyed with my habit of sneaking demons and tiny dragons into the backgrounds of my paintings.

That annoyed instructor taught mural design, and one of our assignments was to design a mural for an elegant hotel dining room. When I filled the wall space with scaly red-eyed grotesque monsters crawling over a rocky landscape Mr. Mayer blew his stack.

"I'm fed up with you!" he exploded. "I've had enough of your lousy monsters puking all over everything!!"

That instructor couldn't squelch my intense enthusiasm for painting, and after school was out in June I continued to paint on into the summer.

I decided to do my painting at my Aunt Ella's farm in Kentucky, just across the Ohio River.

58

I call it Aunt Ella's farm because she ran the place. She had to, since Uncle Frank and his eighty-seven-year-old father, Eli, were so childlike they had to be told what to do every hour of the day.

That farm was only a fraction of the size of Grandfather's, with a small frame house, a ramshackle little barn, and a few acres planted in corn and tobacco.

My first painting was a portrait of old Eli sitting in a chair out in the yard, and not budging an inch, in obedience to Aunt Ella's instructions. I painted him as quickly as possible, since I knew he would much prefer to be out plowing with his thirty-seven-year-old mule, Josephine.

Next I painted a view of Aunt Ella's kitchen with sunlight from a window lending a special radiance to her old cast-iron stove.

Then I painted a gloomy scene of the front porch overgrown with climbing vines and a worn-out old sofa and a chair back in the shadows.

My last canvas was gloomier yet, and perhaps a bit grisly. It was a still life arranged in a corner of the front porch which included a rat in a trap, a lantern, and a pair of old boots.

Near the end of August my cousin Eli, who lived in Detroit, came to visit his parents for a week, and on his return trip he gave me and my pictures a ride back to Indianapolis.

There was just enough time to get the pictures framed and enter them in the Indiana State Fair Art Exhibition. Once they were entered I began to worry. In 1934 no artist could afford to pass up a chance for a cash prize no matter how small, and all the best artists in the state would have their paintings in the show. And when the fair opened in September I was well prepared for a bitter disappointment. Nevertheless, I hurried across the fairgrounds to the art pavilion anxious to see the results, whatever they might be.

The instant I entered the main gallery I spotted old Eli above the heads of the crowd, and on second look I discovered a red ribbon attached to his frame.

It was an overwhelming moment, and to this day it remains one of the biggest thrills in memory.

After I had recovered from my stunning surprise I was delighted to find my other paintings were also on display, even my rat picture.

I'd had misgivings about exhibiting that one, and sure enough it had attracted a hostile crowd wondering why such a frightful picture was ever put on display.

The critics were mostly women, since the men much preferred the livestock, the farm machinery, and the sulky races.

I'd have been greatly upset by all the harsh criticism if I hadn't won the prize for old Eli. Now it was easy to laugh it off, and I returned to the art pavilion many times to linger near the rat picture to enjoy all the fuss and furor my outrageously bad taste had stirred up.

One of my favorite subjects for painting was the big top circus, and whenever a circus came to town I was up at dawn and trotting off to the outskirts of the city to be there when the circus train pulled in. For me the greatest show on earth was the unloading, as six-horse teams hauled the huge circus wagons off the flat cars, the elephants emerged from their cattle cars, and

roustabouts swarmed onto the field with tent poles and rolls of canvas. And in all the confusion and chaos, a great tent city appeared out of nowhere.

I attempted to sketch the big scene many times, but finally realized I couldn't keep dodging horses and roustabouts and sketch at the same time, so I got an eyeful of it all and sketched it later.

My circus paintings were never of the dazzling spectacles in the big tops. Never the high-flying Cadonnas or the Riding Rapinskis or the death-defying high wire acts.

My paintings were about either the great struggle to get the tents up or all the activity in the shadows of the back lot as performers prepared for their entrance into the limelight.

I seemed to be attracted to the gloomy side of things, or the sordid. No vases of flowers or water lilies for me.

66

One of the dreariest of my prize-winning paintings was titled *The Other Side of the Tracks,* a scene of an old shantytown southwest of the city where I'd done some sketching. The picture centered around the forlorn figure of a black man with a hovel of a shack and a switch engine in the background against an eerie evening sky.

My portraits were never of beautiful people. I much preferred to paint grizzled old men improved with time like gnarled oak trees. One of my prize portraits was *Henry,* depicting an old codger living in Margaret's little town of Ladoga. I painted the old fellow as an excuse to visit Margaret, I must admit. When Henry's portrait appeared in the Sunday paper after winning the prize he was a celebrity in Ladoga for months afterward.

As much as I loved the art school I left after three years and set up my easel in an abandoned office building downtown. I was tired of being broke and running out of paint and canvas.

My plan was to divide my time between painting and doing department store ads.

Margaret and I planned to be married as soon as I could make a fairly good income. Unfortunately, the department store ads couldn't be counted on. I might make twenty-five dollars one week and five dollars the next.

68

I completed only one painting in that old building, and it was a farm landscape inspired by my grandfather's austere old mansion and his great barn. To give the picture an extra dimension I put the mansion and the barn on separate hills and added a farmer herding some pigs across the barn lot.

The painting eventually won a two-hundred-dollar prize at the Marshall Field's Gallery in Chicago, but I knew better than to count on painting prizes for a regular income.

Nineteen thirty-seven was a poor year to start a career as a painter, or a career of any kind for that matter. The prevailing mood of that year was gloom and despair.

In early spring the Ohio River flooded, leaving thousands homeless. There was a strike in the auto industry that erupted into bloody violence. Amelia Earhart, the famous pilot, disappeared on a flight over the Pacific and was never heard from again. The main attraction at the newsreel theaters was the horrifying Hindenburg disaster. Unemployment continued to be a national problem with no end of the Depression in sight.

One day when I dropped by the art school to visit friends, the director of the school handed me a brochure from the Walt Disney Studios. "If you're interested," he said, "they need artists out there."

The brochure included an application to fill out, and a variety of action sketches were required.

I enjoyed the Disney films I had seen but was never interested in any kind of cartooning. Yet it was no time to be choosy, so I filled out the application, dashed off the required sketches, and stuck them in the mail.

That spring I left the old building to go job hunting. I had no luck at all in Indianapolis, but when I heard that a greeting card company in Dayton, Ohio, was hiring artists I took the short bus ride there to give it a try.

It turned out to be the simplest of jobs, merely filling in areas of color on other artists' designs. The pay was twenty-five dollars for a six-day week, and for all I could see there was no possible way up from my position. The only thing I liked about the job was my view of a freight yard from my second-story window where switch engines kept chugging back and forth all day.

When the boss announced that we would be doing sympathy cards for the rest of the summer it was too much. My job was already tedious, and touching up delicate flowers would be even more frustrating.

So I took the next bus out of Dayton. When I returned to

Indianapolis there was a special delivery letter waiting for me from Walt Disney Studios. It was a form letter requesting me to report to the studio for a tryout on September 9.

I suspected the Disney Company had sent out hundreds of such invitations, but nevertheless I was willing to try anything if I could only find an inexpensive way to get to California. Margaret solved that problem neatly when she learned that a man from her hometown who was living in Los Angeles was in Indianapolis on business and would be heading home about the same time I needed a ride to Disney.

I met Dave Gill at his hotel and he agreed to give me a ride to Los Angeles for twenty dollars if I would do a share of the driving. It was more of a bargain than I could ever have hoped for, although I *did* worry about the driving part. My driving experience amounted to borrowing the family car three or four times, and the last time I had steered into a curb and blown two tires.

Dave did the driving the first morning, and he spent an hour complaining about how dull and depressing Indiana was. His main complaint was about his breakfast. "Would you believe it?!" he grumped. "They didn't even serve hash browns with my ham and eggs! That is *downright heathenish!!*"

I was resigned to be stuck with an arrogant sorehead for twenty-four hundred miles, but for twenty dollars it was still a terrific bargain. However, when we made our first overnight stop at California, Missouri, of all places, I discovered that Dave was anything but a sorehead. He was a jolly forty-year-old playboy, and he knew some people in the town and was out with friends half the night.

To Dave life was one big party, and while I hit the sack early at every overnight stop Dave sampled the nightlife. That meant that I did the driving in the morning while Dave caught up on his sleep in the back seat.

Highway 40 was a rough, jolting ride in those days, with many deep ditches and potholes, and there were long stretches of gravel that slowed us to a crawl. And to make the going even slower there were long detours taking us far out into the farm country. Between the bad roads and Dave's late morning risings I began to worry about the September 9 date, only a few days away.

When we headed out of Denver up the long grades into the Rockies I worried about Dave's Dodge holding up. We passed many old cars stalled along the roadside with steam spurting out of their radiators while families stood by helplessly. Some of those people were the "Okies" John Steinbeck wrote about in his *Grapes of Wrath* — those who fled the dust bowl hoping to find work in California.

As the going got steeper and the roads twisted up around the mountainsides I was wishing Dave was at the wheel.

The going was made even more treacherous with the road being repaired. Huge bulldozers and oversized dump trucks forced me perilously close to the edges, sometimes less than a foot from thousand-foot drops to the canyons below. I'm sure Dave couldn't have slept soundly if he had been aware of those close calls or known of my limited driving experience. It was a scary four or five hours until we stopped for lunch in a roadside cafe and Dave took over for the afternoon.

We made good time across Utah and Nevada and by Friday evening we were in Las Vegas, which was Dave's kind of town, one that never sleeps. And of course he was out all night and on into the next day.

Just when I was considering hitchhiking the last three hundred miles Dave showed up and flopped down to sleep in the back seat of his trusty Dodge. And on the evening of September 7 we arrived in Los Angeles, although it was hard to tell just where the sprawling city began.

"I hated it when I first came here," Dave said, "but you'll love it once you get used to it." Dave had read my mind. I was appalled at the starkness of the landscape with its tall palms like slightly bent telephone poles with mop tops.

The dry desert heat was oppressive and the hillsides were barren except for patches of wiry crabgrass. The houses were a variety of small tile-roofed bungalows and miniature haciendas overlooking the highway. And looming up in the purplish haze beyond was a jagged mountain range.

I stayed at Dave's apartment Saturday night, and Sunday he dropped me off in front of the Disney Studios.

As Dave left he reminded me to call him if I ran short of money or had any problems. We had become good friends during our trek from Indiana, and it was nice to know I wasn't entirely alone in that foreign land.

The Disney Studios were closed in by a high cement wall, and the only view was through the wrought-iron front gate. What I could see of the complex looked most inviting. There was a flagstone walk across a grass courtyard to an archway in front of what appeared to be the main building—a quaint, cozy look appropriate for a company dealing with fun and fantasy.

80

Just a block from the studios I ran across a rooming house, a big barn of a place with the second floor and the attic sectioned off into narrow compartments with a small cot in each one. The landlady was a little mouse of a woman who explained apologetically that the two dollars a week rent need not be paid until I could afford it.

Her tenants were mostly Disney beginners or else newcomers like me who had no guarantee of a job. That dear little lady, Mrs. Beson, was well aware of our situation, and no doubt she had seen many come and go who could never pay the rent.

The next morning at the appointed time of nine o'clock I was at the Disney front gate. It was the wrong place. I was told to check in at a one-story stucco building across the street called the Disney Annex. The tryout group had already lined up at the front door to sign in, and I was the last of the fifteen to arrive.

Most of them were fresh out of art school as I was, and they came from all parts of the country in response to the special delivery letter, not knowing what to expect.

The boss of the Annex, George Drake, was a tall, scrawny chain-smoking neurotic with a shock of rusty hair and extremely large ears. He started things off with a stern lecture warning us that the one-month tryout would be no bed of roses. And more than once he reminded us how fortunate we were to get an opportunity to work for Disney. "There are plenty of people waiting out on the street to get a job here" was his last warning.

After the lecture we were given model sheets, guides to drawing Mickey, Donald, and Goofy so we could practice the roundish Disney drawing style.

During that one-month period Drake kept us on edge by continually pacing the hall and popping in on us at odd moments. Every few days one or two of the group were let go, and as it came down to the last week we wondered if Drake would fire all of us.

I was warned many times about leaving the buttons off of Mickey's pants, but even so I was one of the three survivors at the end of the month.

We were put to work as in-betweeners, with the tedious, painstaking job of adding hundreds of drawings in between hundreds of other drawings to move Donald or Mickey from here to there.

It was a matter of enduring the job with the hope of making it to the promised land across the street where big exciting things were going on. They were making *Snow White and the Seven Dwarfs,* the very first feature-length animated film.

I wrote to Margaret immediately to let her know I made it
through the tryouts and was on the job. And even though it was
assembly-line work there would be all kinds of opportunities if
Snow White was a success.

I didn't mention all the dire predictions coming from Hollywood
bigwigs and movie columnists. They called *Snow White* Disney's
Folly. The picture would be a box office flop! People would never
sit through a full-length cartoon feature! Disney was getting too
big for his britches! And so on.

Those ominous predictions made me wonder if I had arrived
just in time to board the Disney *Titanic*. And I'm sure those
voices of doom haunted the people working with a frenzy to
complete *Snow White* in time for the grand première before
Christmas. I even got in on the last-minute effort, working nights
tracing dwarves on something called a rotoscope machine.

Margaret came out on the train the last week of November and we were married on the thirtieth, then moved into a dingy little apartment about a half-hour walk from the studio.

A few weeks later, we attended the gala première of *Snow White*. All Disney employees and their wives or husbands were invited, along with hundreds of special guests and newspeople. As we moved through the mob toward the marquee of the Carthay Circle Theater, I caught my first glimpse of Walt Disney. He was addressing the crowd from a podium, but his voice was lost in all the hubbub.

Very few people who worked on the film had seen it all in one piece, so it was a new experience for most of the audience. Of course the overwhelming success of *Snow White* is motion picture history, and as I write about it now, it is out in the theaters for the seventh time, having celebrated its fiftieth anniversary in 1987.

86

I believe everyone in that first *Snow White* audience could have predicted the enormous success of the film. They were carried away by the picture from the very beginning, and as it went along everyone was bubbling over with enthusiasm and frequently bursting into spontaneous applause. At the end, the audience exploded into a thunderous ovation—and the voices of doom were silenced for good.

It was a tremendous triumph for Walt Disney, and as Margaret and I left the theater on that balmy December night I felt as if I were part of it—a wonderful feeling that lasted until the following Monday morning.

Like a drawing robot I in-betweened Donald Ducks by the hundreds eight hours a day. And to make the job even more exasperating George Drake kept hounding me to pick up the pace.

Some of the in-betweeners had been at the job for years with no hope of anything better. But then there was no way to prove you could do anything else as long as you were limited to in-betweening. And the pay would never be much better than the twenty-two dollars and fifty cents a week I started with.

I did manage to make a few extra dollars by responding to mimeographed sheets circulated through the studio requesting gags or ideas for stories which were in the planning stage. If any of your ideas were accepted, you might be paid as much as five dollars.

One day the mimeographed sheet requested ideas for *Pinocchio,* the new cartoon feature in the works. They wanted sketches of zany, imaginative monsters to inhabit a place called Bogyland.

If there was ever a chance to prove what I could do this was it. At last the time for my monsters had come!

I spent night after night working in a frenzy in our apartment with colored pencils turning out pages and pages of all the zaniest, goofiest monsters I could dream up. Then I stuffed them into a large envelope and took them back to the Annex to be delivered to the story department, somewhere across the street.

After a couple of weeks without any word about my bogies I dismissed the effort as a total loss and began to worry about how much longer I could endure in-betweening the devilish ducks. After drawing him a few thousand times I had begun to despise Donald.

Finally, one unseasonably warm afternoon in March, another great stack of duck drawings arrived to be in-betweened. It was too much! I went berserk and shouted at the top of my voice, "*NO MORE DUCKS!!!*" much to the horror of my fellow in-be-tweeners.

"Bill, Bill," some of them whispered, "take it easy. You'll blow the whole thing." Blowing the whole thing was exactly what I meant to do, once and for all. And I went charging out of the room and on down the hall shouting *"NO MORE DUCKS! NO MORE LOUSY DUCKS!"* I kept on shouting as I passed Drake's office and went storming on out of the Annex.

Then over the hills and on back to our apartment I went, condemning Donald Duck and George Drake to the depths of purgatory all the way.

When I told Margaret of my Donald Duck Tantrum she wasn't the least bit perturbed. "Why don't we go to New York?" she said. "That's where you wanted to go in the first place."

As we sat there wondering how we could ever make it to New York it suddenly occurred to me that I had left my jacket draped on the back of my chair in the Annex. Seedy and worn out as it was the jacket was the only one I had, and I couldn't afford a new one.

The next morning I reluctantly returned to the scene of my crime, and as I crept in the front door and down the hall the Annex was as quiet as a graveyard—with no sign of George Drake anywhere. And the in-betweeners gave me the old silent treatment as I retrieved my precious jacket.

As I made a hasty exit I snatched an envelope off my drawing table which was addressed to me. It was sure to be a dismissal notice and yet curiosity prevailed, so once I was safely outside on the sidewalk I opened it.

Sure enough, there *was* a pink slip in the envelope, but nothing like a dismissal notice. It was a memo requesting that I report to the story department. Also there was a check for twenty-five dollars in payment for my bogies. My monsters had come through just in the nick of time! What a marvelous surprise! It was comparable to the thrill of seeing old Eli at the fair with a red ribbon stuck on his frame.

Feeling twenty feet tall I marched across the street and presented my memo to the gateman, and he directed me to the story department, which was past the main building, across a parking lot, in an old stucco apartment house.

The old building had been acquired as Disney was enlarging his story staff for feature-length films. The story crews occupied all of the living rooms, bedrooms, dining rooms, and kitchenettes of the two-story building. I was to report to Leo Ellis, a story man in one of the second-floor bedrooms who was working on the Bogyland section of *Pinocchio*.

Leo was originally from somewhere in the Midwest and had "gone Hollywood," which included dark glasses, scarf tucked into his shirt front, baggy pants, leather sandals, and a long cigarette holder.

Leo already had another sketch man, Don DaGradi, working for him, so Don and I shared the job of filling the story boards with dancing bogies.

Story boards are four-by-eight-foot panels, and a continuity of sketches is pushpinned onto the boards to show the main phases of the action and the personalities and attitudes of the characters as a plan for the animation.

As the story man, Leo was the brain who supplied us with ideas on how we were to illustrate the boards.

96

But he hardly ever discussed Bogyland with us. He preferred
to reminisce about his youthful escapades way back during his
high school years.

Now and then Leo talked of the glorious future for the Walt
Disney Studios and all the great opportunities ahead.

"Don, my lad," he would say, "Disney will be doing great things,
and you and I will be in on it. Just think—how lucky we are."

Leo never included me in that glorious future. As far as he
was concerned I wasn't even there. So I was greatly relieved
when Don and I had filled the walls of the bedroom with dancing
bogies and I was sent off to sketch for another story man in a
bedroom down the hall.

Al Geise was a plump, owlish little man with bulging, soft-boiled eyes. His assignment was a brief episode showing the old toy maker Geppetto out to sea in a small sailboat searching for Pinocchio, who is captive on an island. Suddenly the old fellow, boat and all, is swallowed in one great gulp by Monstro the Whale.

Al always started the day complaining about his various ailments, describing his aches and pains in meticulous detail. After that he turned to everyone's favorite topic, Walt Disney. In Al's opinion Walt was an insensitive, uncultured, illiterate clod. A Kansas City hayseed. A tyrant and a bully, and on and on.

Al's opinion of Walt would have been disturbing if I had taken him seriously, but miserable Al seemed to be at odds with the world in general.

Hearing the old-timers talk about Walt was much more enlightening. They were laughing all the way as they recounted the early days, ten years earlier, when the studio staff was small, and like a family affair they got together on weekends for picnics and games in the park.

When it came to softball games Walt was so fiercely competitive it was laughable. All the players on both sides were Disney employees, and so were the umpires. When Walt came to bat he was sure to get a hit one way or another. If he dribbled the ball back to the mound the pitcher threw wild, far beyond the first baseman's reach. If Walt sent a lazy pop fly to the outfield the fielders invariably bobbled it. When Walt came sliding home he was nearly always called safe. If he was called out, Walt was furious. Of course Walt seldom struck out.

One day the country club atmosphere of the old apartment house was shattered when Otto Englander, the supervising director of *Pinocchio,* announced that Walt wanted to see the whole thing, and as soon as possible.

Suddenly the place was humming with activity as all the story men frantically checked their boards, hoping to make last-minute improvements. The fear of Walt was all too evident in the frenzy the announcement caused.

Al was the most frantic of the lot. He had me redoing drawings by the dozen for no apparent reason. Then at the last moment he smudged all my skies with his sweaty fingers to increase the gloominess of the frightful episode.

Al was still messing up my skies when the traffic boys arrived to carry the boards over to the main building.

There must have been at least seventy story boards to tell that first version of *Pinocchio*. The conference was scheduled for nine o'clock, and about fifteen minutes ahead of time the story men followed by the sketch men straggled across the parking lot to the main building, then down a long hall to sweat box four, the largest of the projection rooms. Directors, assistant directors, layout artists, and songwriters arrived from other parts of the studio and took their seats according to rank, with the story sketch men bringing up the rear. Front and center was an armchair waiting for Walt.

There was a lot of nervous chattering as the sweat box clock inched around toward nine, and as it reached the hour a deep silence set in. The silence was interrupted by the jangle of the telephone. It was Delores, Walt's secretary, calling to tell us he would be about ten minutes late. Even in those days, long before TV shows and Disneyland, Walt's schedule was overbooked. Delores called two or three more times to inform us of delays before Walt's long striding footsteps echoed far down the hall, a man in a hurry who burst into the sweat box full speed with a cheery "Hi Guys!" which brought an enthusiastic chorus of "Hi Walt!" from the assemblage.

"Everybody here?" he asked as he plunked down into his chair.

"All here!" we replied.

"Then let's get the thing started," Walt said.

A story man quickly stepped forward with pointer in hand to explain the opening sequence of *Pinocchio,* and the two-day session was under way.

The first boards showed Geppetto the old toy maker putting the finishing touches on a puppet. When he notices a bright star out the window he makes a wish: he wishes for a son, and out of the star comes the good fairy.

Walt interrupted at this point and said, "Couldn't we use a song in here?"

"How about that little verse?" someone said: " 'Star light, star bright. Make my wish come true tonight.' "

Leigh Harlene, a songwriter, latched onto the idea and in a week or two "When You Wish Upon a Star" was born.

As the conference continued through the morning the jovial Walt who greeted us earlier was getting more cantankerous by the minute.

"There's too much stuff here," he kept complaining. Now and then he would step up to a board and rip off a whole row of sketches.

Walt was tough and businesslike as he leaned out on the edge of his chair scowling at the boards. The atmosphere was getting pretty grim until Honest John Foulfellow, a villainous fox, was introduced on the boards. Walt's mood changed in a flash and suddenly he was the sly, debonair fox, overacting the part to perfection.

After seeing the gruff, overbearing Walt it was a refreshing turnabout to see the playful Walt in action. His exaggerated attitudes were truly funny and he had us laughing all the way. Exaggeration is the very essence of animation, so necessary to creating larger-than-life personalities.

After the fox performance Walt reverted to his bearish ways, grumbling about all the surplus material, all the wasted time and money. Leo didn't make it halfway through his presentation of Bogyland before Walt called a halt.

"We don't need all this stuff," he grumped. "Too much!" So it was goodbye bogies, every last one.

Al was the most jittery performer of the lot and nearly lost his voice as he stammered through our seagoing epic to the final great "GULP."

Walt didn't hesitate a minute in dismissing the thing. "That's too scary," he said. "Don't you think we could explain this some other way?"

"Yes, Walt!" was the unanimous verdict, and poor Al was crushed.

Walt must have eliminated more than half the story boards before he called an end to the story conference, and as he was about to leave he turned to us with a satisfied smile and said, "That was a hell of a good session." It left me wondering what a bad one would be like.

Much later I would appreciate Walt's efforts during that two-day story conference—his uncanny ability to evaluate, to separate the wheat from the chaff.

I also got an idea of how opinions of Walt were formed. Those who had fared well at the conference and came out with their boards intact praised Walt to the skies. He was a great guy! A remarkable man! A great talent! A genius! Meanwhile, the disgruntled losers echoed Al's negative opinions. Of course those opinions could change from month to month according to their successes or failures.

There was a shakeup the following week and the *Pinocchio* crew was reduced considerably. Al was sent off to work on *Bambi*. And Leo? I can't recall what happened to him. I remained on *Pinocchio* for another year and a half, sketching for many story men working on nearly every section of the story.

Walt recognized my drawings as being "great stuff" on many occasions, and my drawings *did* have something to do with the final versions of the characters. And I even put ideas of my own into the story while I did the sketching.

It occurred to me that I was well suited for the Disney job, and I had thought of making a career of it until Margaret and I attended the special *Pinocchio* preview for the Disney staff.

I was dumbfounded when the long list of screen credits didn't include my name.

108

Being left off the credits made me realize I was still just another sketch man, just one of the mob, and I was depressed for weeks afterward. And when I was assigned to sketch on *Fantasia* I was even more discouraged when I joined fourteen other sketch men to create a pictorial version of Beethoven's Fifth Symphony.

While the record player filled the rooms with Beethoven we filled the boards with flying horses, centaurs, centaurettes, fauns, and cherubs, flying, galloping, and dancing all over the Olympian landscape. The story men were at a loss to tell us what to do, so we were responsible for what finally came out on the screen.

Meanwhile Walt was having a big new studio built out in a place called the San Fernando Valley, near the town of Burbank. During the construction Walt drove us out to see it a group at a time.

Walt was excited about the new building even though it was out in a treeless wasteland of nothing but tumbleweeds.

Nevertheless, when Walt asked what we thought of it our reply was "Great, Walt!"

It would take awhile to get used to the modern building with all new furniture, especially after feeling so much at home in the old run-down apartment house with faded wallpaper and tattered window shades. Artists need an atmosphere of poverty, a degree of shabbiness to get into a creative mood.

110

The intimidating big business atmosphere of the new building became much less difficult for me when I was assigned to work on *Dumbo,* the story of the little circus elephant with the enormous floppy ears.

Otto Englander, the supervisor of *Dumbo,* was familiar with my work on *Pinocchio* and gave me a large part of the story to develop on my own.

The year and a half I spent on *Dumbo* was a happy time, especially since our first son, Bill, was born just the year before I went to work on the picture, and my infant son was a definite influence in the way I drew the baby elephant.

With all my years of sketching and painting the circus I was well prepared for *Dumbo,* and I contributed so much to the production that Otto allowed me to present my story boards to Walt one day.

In facing Walt for the first time I understood why many story men became so nervous and shaky they often lost their voices. It was an unnerving experience to concentrate on the boards while Walt leaned forward in his chair as if he were ready to pounce.

His fierce scowl was also disconcerting even though it was usually a sign of deep concentration.

I was greatly relieved to make it through the boards without faltering and find Walt relaxed and smiling.

But then Walt was enthusiastic about all my boards on *Dumbo,* and I thought sure I was established as a full-fledged story man on films to come. No such luck!

113

When I was assigned to sketch on *Peter Pan* for Mr. T., another story man, I realized I was going nowhere. Mr. T. was a plump, jovial fellow who was most agreeable to leaving the whole job up to me, the story work as well as the sketching, while he was either on the phone or out in the hall in search of a conversation.

At such times I needed to remind myself of George Drake and the Annex experience to control my anger.

So I worked out a section of *Peter Pan* with as much enthusiasm as I could manage under the conditions, and when the boards were ready Mr. T. presented them to Walt with his own special flair and flamboyance.

The only thing that could free me from Mr. T. was a war. And when the Japanese bombed Pearl Harbor we were jolted out of Never-Never Land into the horrifying reality of World War II. Almost overnight the fantasy factory was totally involved in the war effort, producing training films, propaganda films to sell war bonds, and films to vilify and ridicule the enemy.

Army and navy brass paraded up and down the halls as authorities and supervisors on the various government projects, and Walt was no longer commander in chief. I worked on a great variety of films during the war years, sometimes under a story man and sometimes on my own. I remember drawing dozens of goofy Hitlers, bulldoggish Mussolinis, and monstrous, evil-looking enemy war machines of all kinds.

One of the projects was *Education for Death*, showing the German youth being trained from early childhood to become Nazi storm troopers.

Walt's pet project was *Victory through Air Power*, based on Major Alexander de Seversky's book promoting long-range bombing as the key to victory.

I was assigned to illustrate a brief episode for that documentary feature: it was the bombing of New York City by enemy aircraft to show what could happen if they beat us to the punch.

I bombed New York with great reluctance. After all, the war
was still going full blast and an American city being blown out
of sight was a very real possibility.

My treatment of the episode was simple. I started off with
waves of enemy bombers roaring out of an eerie dawn sky and
on over the sleeping city, with the skyscrapers in dark silhouette.
Then, as the aircraft pass over their target, bomb bays fly open
and the deadly eggs rain down.

The explosions rock the city and the skyscrapers tumble down
to disappear in billowing clouds of smoke. Then the smoke drifts
away, revealing the awful devastation.

118

The last scenes are of the Statue of Liberty sinking into the dark, murky waters of the harbor. As the torch disappears all is quiet.

When Walt took a look at it he said, "You *really* did it, didn't you Bill?!"

"I'm afraid so," I said, feeling a bit guilty.

"I don't think we need this," he said, turning to the group in attendance.

"*No, Walt!!*" was the emphatic response from all, including Major de Seversky. And for the first time I was happy to see one of my boards get the old thumbs down.

Air power did indeed prove to be the dominant force in our victories over Germany and Japan, but no one, not even Major de Seversky, could foresee the magnitude of the big one dropped on Hiroshima which would change the world forever.

Shaking off the dreary mood of the war was like coming out of a bad dream, and it took awhile for the funny factory to get back to business as usual. The Disney feature films made just before the war didn't come close to returning the millions invested in them, and making another one was questionable.

Nevertheless, the irrepressible Mr. Disney took a big leap into a live action feature. It was *Song of the South,* featuring the legendary Uncle Remus relating his old folktales about Br'er Rabbit, Br'er Fox, and Br'er Bear.

The folktales were to be animated segments within the live action story, coming to life as Uncle Remus tells them to a small boy. When Walt handed me the job of planning the Remus tales, I was both delighted and befuddled. Was I a story man once and for all? Or just for a while? Anyway, developing the characters of the rabbit, the fox, and the bear and working with the quaint old fables was the most fun I'd had since *Dumbo.*

In the story conferences I had attended, I had seen the grumpy, bearish Walt and the jovial, good-natured one, and you could never be sure which Walt to expect. On the Remus fables, Walt was always in a good humor, full of enthusiasm at every story session, and the animators caught the playful spirit in preparing the fables for the screen.

Walt was quick to categorize people, and if you were good at drawing that meant you were deficient in most other respects. So I do believe I convinced him on the Uncle Remus fables that I was a sketch man who could also handle the story end of it.

Song of the South was fairly successful and yet it had little effect on the deficit caused by the losses at the box office in previous years. Once again Walt was faced with the big question: Do we dare invest in another feature film?

Walt was the bear in those worrisome times, always in a growling mood and hard to deal with. The guys, as he called us, had no idea the studio was on thin ice. After all, Walt didn't have to be worried to be in a grumpy mood. When Walt insisted the studio invest in one more cartoon feature, his brother, Roy, who handled the money end of the business, disagreed. He was all for picking up their marbles and retiring in comfort. They argued fiercely for two weeks until Roy reluctantly gave in. Then Walt chose *Cinderella* as the best bet for their money.

The familiar story of *Cinderella* is so simple that it is often told on one or two pages in collections of fairy tales. To develop the story into a feature lasting an hour and twenty minutes called for enlarging the plot and creating additional characters. Walt assigned me the job of creating a small army of mice and a villainous cat, and I couldn't have been happier, even though inventing new mice and a new cat wouldn't be easy since there had been so many varieties of them in comic strips and animated films.

The drawings on these pages were taken from photostats of mice I drew in 1947, before I began to work on the story boards.

Jaq, a scrawny little mouse, and Gus, a plump, slow-witted one, played major roles in the picture, and their heroics in out-smarting the villainous cat, Lucifer, were crucial to *Cinderella*'s happy ending. And when the picture made it big at the box office, it was indeed *Walt's* Cinderella story, making it possible for him to keep his dreams alive, which included Disneyland.

After my work on *Cinderella* my job at the studio was beginning to show promise, and yet I knew better than to take my success for granted. Sooner or later my Disney career would come to an end and I would need to make a living at something else. I hoped I could make it as a painter.

I had been planning a number of paintings in miniature, hoping to enlarge them on canvas during weekends. If I could complete enough of them, I hoped to have a one-man show at a Los Angeles art gallery to gain some recognition and eventually sell some of them.

For my first full-size painting, I selected a scene of a train heading into the sunset with an old barn and a horse in the foreground. It was the train that ran past Aunt Ella's farm every evening at dinner time.

Once I began to paint I realized to my dismay I had lost touch with the brush, and the results were dull and uninspired. Nevertheless, I was determined to complete the picture no matter what, and I kept working on it during the weekends until I was ready for the final details. By that time, I had lost interest in the gloomy scene and wondered whether it was worth finishing. My son Bill spared me that decision one afternoon when my studio door was left open.

He put the final touch on the picture with one of my larger brushes, a broad zinc white scriggle across the lower half of the canvas.

When Margaret discovered Billy's wild zigzag of a scriggle, she was horrified and she worried about how devastated I would be. But to her surprise I burst out laughing. What a relief it was to say goodbye to the evening train and the whole idea of painting as a second career.

130

During the years I had been working for Disney the world of fine art had changed drastically, and after making the rounds of the art galleries and museums in the Los Angeles area, Margaret and I realized my American scenes were as extinct as dinosaurs. So I put my brushes and palette aside and turned to the drawing board for a try at magazine cartoons as a possible second career.

I kept scratching away with pen and ink in the evenings and on through the weekends turning out what I hoped were funny cartoons, some with captions and some purely visual gags. As I illustrated one idea after another, I questioned if any of them were funny or even slightly amusing.

The humor I had put into the Disney films had brought laughs in the theaters, and sometimes even explosions of laughter, which was proof I could be funny in the animated pictures. I must have made more than a hundred drawings attempting to be funny and at the same time to develop a distinctive style. All of the best-known cartoonists had unique styles that could be recognized at a glance.

I CAN'T QUITE PUT A FINGER ON IT, BUT YOUR CHILD
STRIKES ME AS AN ODD ONE.

When I had finally exhausted my supply of "funny" ideas, I selected what I considered to be some of the best cartoons and sent them off to the magazines. The cartoons on these pages are a few of those early experiments I found stuck in my files, having gathered dust over the past forty years.

133

BARBARA, BEFORE WE GET BETTER ACQUAINTED THERE
IS SOMETHING YOU SHOULD KNOW—
I'M REALLY NOT WEARING SWIM FINS.

IT'S THE ENGLISH CHANNEL! WE'RE SPLASHIN'
HER DOWN JUST OUTSIDE PHOENIX!

I WANT A GOOD CLEAN FIGHT—NO CLINCHIN', NO
HITTIN' ON THE BREAK, NO BUTTIN'— AN' NO RABBIT
PUNCHIN'.

134

SORRY, SIR, I'M AFRAID THAT'S ALL WE HAVE IN PIGSKIN.

DO YOU EVER GET THOSE STRANGE, HOPELESS, SORT OF
EMPTY FEELINGS?

I sent them to *Colliers, True Magazine,* the *Post,* and the *New Yorker,* and in each case they were returned with a routine rejection slip. The one note of encouragement was attached to the *New Yorker* rejection: "Your humor is too undisciplined, but we would like to see more of your drawings." That small glimmer of hope wasn't nearly enough to spur me on. Doing cartoons week after week, even if I sold them all, would be frustrating work.

I was much more interested in illustrating story books, which was my very first boyhood ambition. And after working on stories for Disney, I also had thoughts about writing them. By this time Billy was about eight and our second son, Steve, was four, and almost every night at bedtime I made up a story for them. Those storytelling hours were wonderful fun, and their enthusiasm and gleeful responses to my stories made me wonder if other kids might enjoy them too.

Before I could plan any storybooks, there was the problem of writing them, which would take some doing.

137

My Disney storytelling had been a series of sketches, hundreds of them to describe every phase of the action and the attitudes of the characters. The only words needed were the lines of dialogue printed below the sketches.

It was impossible to put aside the drawing habit long enough to do much writing. I hardly ever wrote more than a paragraph before my wayward pen wandered off into a drawing. As I continued to dream up stories on large tablets, the pages were filled with drawings of characters with very little room for words.

"Lambert the Sheepish Lion" was one of my very first attempts at a story. It was about a lion cub delivered by the stork to a mother sheep by mistake. Lambert grows up to be a hero and pride of the flock.

138

Then there was a story about a little car, an "auto-biography" you might say. A typical life of a car from showroom to used car lot to junkyard to hot rod.

"Goliath II" was about a tiny elephant no more than five inches tall, who was a problem for his mother but of special interest to old Rajah the tiger, who had never tasted an elephant.

"Homer" was the story of a country bumpkin of a pigeon who is talked into going to the big city by a sparrow and runs into all kinds of trouble. "Smokey" was about a little switch engine who puffs smoke rings and after a near disastrous adventure is able to puff smoke in all sorts of shapes.

"No Such Things" was a collection of nonsensical creatures I dreamed up just for the fun of it.

Another story starts off with a lion's mane catching fire—his problem is to grow a new one. "The Pinkish, Purplish, Bluish Egg" was no more than a dove trying to hatch a huge egg with the title printed below.

"Ella" was a spoiled prima donna of a circus elephant who runs away and is finally unspoiled by a tyrant of a farmer.

There was another car named Jennifer who was adopted by Josephine, an alley cat, and another train story about unhappy Katy Caboose, who disliked jolting along at the tail end of the train under a cloud of smelly black smoke.

I could visualize the characters and also picture the stories from beginning to end, but when it came to writing them I was at a loss for words.

If I couldn't write the stories, then my characters couldn't go anywhere and would be stranded on my dog-eared old tablets forever. I resisted the temptation to draw and stuck to writing, filling tablet after tablet in my efforts to find the right words. I spent hours every evening trying one story after another, with the same flat, uninspired results.

Even when I was on vacation trips with Margaret and our sons, I continued to work on my writing problem, filling more tablets with my stilted, lifeless prose wherever we went. The results were never more than a jumble of phrases, and I never came close to completing a story.

Very often I went on vacation with Disney problems haunting me and returned from these trips with my tablet filled with notes and sketches concerning *Peter Pan, Alice in Wonderland,* or whatever my assignment might be at the time. The Disney job came first since it brought in a good income. Finally, I gave up the idea of writing storybooks and put my tablets on the shelf along with my stack of magazine cartoons.

Alice in Wonderland was the animated feature Walt selected to follow *Cinderella*. In an effort to make sense out of Alice's adventures, Walt hired experienced screenwriters and play-wrights. The results were usually weighty manuscripts, much more than Walt had the patience to read. Finally the studio story crews were given the job of translating Lewis Carroll's esoteric humor and word play into visual, understandable terms.

Alice in Wonderland was a complicated venture since Alice met such a great variety of characters and became involved in so many nonsensical situations. It was difficult to squeeze the story into an hour and twenty-five minutes.

One Sunday, I went over to the studio to complete one of the Alice episodes while I had it well in mind. While I was working on the sketches, far down the hall echoed those long striding footsteps and Walt's familiar cough. We always assumed Walt's cough was a warning designed to prevent him from surprising anyone who might be goofing off. Walt would be more embarrassed than they were.

That day it wasn't a warning cough because he didn't expect anyone to be there. He came into my room and found me sitting there. He was flabbergasted.

"What—what the devil are you doin' here?!!" he stammered. "Workin'. What are you doing here?" I asked. As I recall he had no reply. Walt was too embarrassed for words, and after staring at my boards for a brief moment, he was gone. I knew of Walt's routine of making the rounds of the studio on Sundays to catch up on things, and I had caught him spying on me.

147

After *Alice,* Walt decided to make another try at *Peter Pan,* which had been shelved at the start of World War II. Walt was evidently determined to convert all the children's classics into Disney films, either in animation or live action.

Peter Pan was much more appropriate for animation than *Alice* had been. It was a fantasy-filled adventure with plenty of action and a variety of characters. The weakness of the story was Peter Pan himself, who was much too arrogant and egocentric to be likable.

His ability to fly and his cleverness take most of the suspense out of his duel with his age-old enemy, Captain Hook. Yet if we made Peter Pan awkward and less of a superboy, he wouldn't have been Peter Pan.

The picture didn't do well at the box office, but like most of the Disney cartoon features it would be rereleased many times, returning the original production cost and millions more.

When it came to doing *Sleeping Beauty,* Walt had too many projects to keep track of. He was like a ringmaster directing a twenty-ring circus. There were the live action features, the true life adventures, the TV shows, and, above all, Disneyland, which had outgrown his most extravagant dreams.

Walt the bear was the one who came to our story conferences, and he usually came in with a scowl and left with a growl.

The most fun I had with *Sleeping Beauty* was inventing a band of monstrous little demons to serve as henchmen for the awesome witch Maleficent.

150

My fun was over when I incurred the wrath of Walt on the
"boy meets girl" sequence, in which a group of forest creatures
manipulate the prince and princess into dancing together. Walt
was dissatisfied with it at the first presentation, and when he
returned a week later to find I hadn't changed it, he was furious.
"I couldn't find a better way of doing it," I explained, "so why
make an arbitrary change?" "The trouble with you," Walt
growled, "is that you've got a mental block."

The next day I was sent down to the main floor to work on Peter Pan peanut butter TV commercials, which was without a doubt my punishment for what Walt considered stubbornness. Nevertheless, that sequence of *Sleeping Beauty* ended up on the screen just as I had first conceived it — so evidently other people, including Walt, were hampered by mental blocks.

I toughed it out for about two months on peanut butter commercials, then stubbornly decided to return to my room, 3B8, on the third floor, whether Walt liked it or not. The room was undisturbed, my desk cluttered with a mess of paper and miscellany, just as I had left it.

But now that I was back, I was in need of a job. And out of desperation I decided to sacrifice one of my stories I had stashed away at home, the story of Goliath II, the tiny five-inch-tall elephant.

The morning I brought the outline of the story with rough sketches to the studio, I ran into Walt in the hall and he stopped to take a look at it. "Cute story," he said as he handed it back to me. "Why don't we make a film out of it?"

With so much on his mind, I do believe Walt had forgotten about kicking me downstairs—at least he didn't bother to mention it. So I went happily ahead to develop Goliath into an animated special. I also made a little Golden Book out of it—*too* little, a disappointing twenty-two pages.

154

It finally occurred to me that as long as it was Walt Disney's "Goliath II," I could write it. But when it came to doing a book for myself, I could never complete one.

It was time I completed a book all my own with no strings attached. I selected "The Adventures of Hubert," about a much too proud lion. When his mane catches fire he jumps into a creek. He saves himself but ends up minus his mane. I spent every spare moment writing "Hubert" bit by bit on small tablets. I even had the audacity to try it in verse. My only previous experience in versifying had been writing birthday cards for Margaret.

Once the writing was complete, I made a variety of illustrations to go with it, and then Margaret typed it for me. She also changed the title to "Hubert's Hair-Raising Adventure," which was perfect for a story about a lion who has the difficult problem of growing a new mane.

After sending it off to a publisher, I wondered if my kind of humor would be funny to anyone in the book business, especially after the dismal results of my magazine cartoons. When "Hubert" was returned with a rejection slip I was indignant.

I couldn't believe my lion story wasn't fit to print. So I stuck "Hubert" back in the mail at least three more times. At last the Houghton Mifflin Company, of Boston, agreed to publish him. In September 1959 *Hubert's Hair-Raising Adventure* went to press.

Discovering copies of *Hubert* on the shelves of a local bookstore was an ecstatic moment. However, it was much too soon to celebrate, since one book in print was a small beginning and a long way from a second career.

When I first came to the story department I was warned, "Once you get in Walt's doghouse, you may never get out." Evidently I *was* in Walt's doghouse. My assignments were no longer on the feature pictures, and after "Goliath II" went into animation, I continued to work on the short films and also planned a number of Walt's early TV shows. The tight deadlines on the television work spoiled any chance of doing it well—once Walt compared the TV projects to pounding sand down a rat hole.

Even though the short films were a step down from the feature-length films, it was a relief to be working on a smaller scale with the end in sight. It was also fun for a change to be doing stories that were intended mostly for laughs. I created a number of stories for Goofy shorts: "Tiger Trouble," "Knight for a Day," "California or Bust," "How to Play Football," and "African Diary."

159

I also planned short films based on storybooks, like Virginia Lee Burton's gem of a book *The Little House* and Robert Lawson's *Ben and Me,* the story of Amos Mouse, who was the brain behind Benjamin Franklin's remarkable accomplishments. It seemed ironic to be converting written words into pictures while my efforts at home were just the opposite: searching for the right words to go with my pictures.

Then I put a couple of my homegrown originals on the boards: "Lambert the Sheepish Lion" and the "Auto-Biography," which I retitled "Susie the Little Blue Coupe" to Disneyfy it. Those five- or six-minute short films called for squeezing a lot of action and fun into a couple of story boards. But it was valuable practice for someone interested in doing children's books with a limited number of pages.

One evening I doodled a gigantic rabbit as big as a horse on my tablet, then wondered what his problems might be if he lived out in the farm country. I called him Huge Harold and I described in verse his narrow escapes as he runs for his life all the way to a happy ending—and a happy beginning when Harold went to press in 1961.

Two books in over two years was slow progress and still a long way from making it as an author, and I was resigned to staying at Disney and doing more and more short subjects and TV shows.

Then one day a book was delivered to my room. In thumbing through the pages of *The Hundred and One Dalmatians*, I could see it was a dog story and I was wondering who could have sent it when I was surprised by a phone call from Walt. "Hey, Bill," he said, "why don't you read that book and let me know what you think? It might make a good animated feature."

After reading it I could see immediately why Walt considered the story good material for animation. First of all, there was an army of sympathetic characters: the Dalmatian puppies and a variety of other dogs.

It was also an unpredictable, suspenseful story, and what made it go was a fiendish witch of a woman, Cruella de Ville, who has the bizarre idea of stealing Dalmatians to make fur coats out of their skins. Then there were Cruella's two moronic stooges, Horace and Jasper, who play a big part as dognappers.

Walt wanted me to plan the whole thing: write a detailed screenplay, do all the story boards, and record voices for all the characters. That had been a job for at least forty people on *Pinocchio* in 1938, but if Walt thought I could do it, then of course there was no question about it.

With no intention of becoming a writer, I had never learned to type. I scrawled my manuscript for *Dalmatians* on large yellow tablets and worked at it with a frenzy every day and on through the weekends. I left out some parts of Dodie Smith's book and enlarged on others without losing the strange twists and turns in the wildly suspenseful story.

165

In about two months, I completed my script, had it typed, put it in a folder, then sent it to Walt. Early the next day, a happy Walt called me into his office to tell me that my script was "great stuff" and I could get going on the story boards. At last, I was out of Walt's doghouse and, by peculiar coincidence, up to my ears in dogs. The story board work would require more than two thousand drawings, not including the hundreds of preliminary sketches. My Disney job was suddenly bigger than ever and to give any thought to my books during off hours was out of the question.

When I recall my time on *Dalmatians* it brings to mind a mystery that puzzles me to this day. It was a week when Walt was in St. John's Hospital out in Santa Monica being checked for kidney stones when I went to Hollywood for lunch with my friend Don DaGradi. On the way there, Don decided to pick up some photos at a small camera store.

Before the store owner could locate Don's prints, he excused himself to answer the phone in the back room. In a few seconds he was back with an annoyed look on his face. "Is one of you Bill Peet?" he asked. "That's me," I replied. "Well, there's a guy on the phone who says he's Walt Disney—wants to talk to you."

When I picked up the phone in the dark storeroom crammed with crates and boxes, I said "Walt, is that you?" "Bill," he said, "I'm going through hell out here. There must be a better way of doin' this. Anyway, I just wanted to tell you to keep goin'. You seem to know what you're doin'."

I expressed my sympathy and thanked him for his vote of confidence, but with no thought of asking him how on earth he had located me. And Don was just as perplexed as I was since he couldn't recall telling anyone he would be stopping off at a camera store. None of the secretaries had an answer to the mystery either. Walt was a wizard, that's all there was to it.

167

If Walt wasn't a wizard, at least he was remarkably intuitive. How else could he have known I was capable of writing a feature-length screenplay? It was a wonder I could write much more than my own name after drawing and daydreaming through my English classes in grade school and high school. I do believe what gave me the language was my love of books and the hours of reading many of the best authors over the years, starting with those animal books at the neighborhood library.

When I suggested that we do a feature based on T. H. White's *The Sword in the Stone,* a fanciful version of the boyhood of King Arthur, Walt was all for it. But once again he insisted I write a screenplay before starting the story board work. Walt the wizard never knew that I patterned Merlin the magician after him when I wrote the script.

168

In his book, T. H. White describes the wizard as a crusty old curmudgeon, argumentative and temperamental, playful at times, and extremely intelligent. Walt was not quite a curmudgeon and he had no beard, but he was a grandfather and much more of a character, and in my drawings of Merlin, I even borrowed Walt's nose.

The Sword in the Stone was complicated, with the Arthurian legend woven into a mixture of other legends and myths. Getting a more direct story line called for a lot of sifting and sorting. Walt questioned the first version of my screenplay, pointing out that it should have had more substance. So I made an all-out effort to give it more substance by enlarging on the more dramatic aspects of the story.

I took the revised script to Walt on a Friday afternoon and he promised to read it in Palm Springs, where he often spent his weekends. Sunday morning, my son Bill called me to the phone. "It's Walt Disney," he said in a whisper. "Walt?" I said into the phone. "Yeah, Bill. I've just read your new script and I like it. I thought I'd let you know so you wouldn't have to worry about it the whole weekend."

I do believe I knew Walt about as well as any employee could know him, even though he was never the same two days in a row. One day he came into my room and slumped down in a chair with a mournful sigh. "What's on your mind, Walt?" I asked. "It gets lonely around here," he said. "I just want to talk to somebody." Then, like a hurt little boy, he poured out the story of his miserable childhood, mostly about selling newspapers for his tyrant of a father, who was a distributor and kept every cent Walt made to pay for his room and board. I was eager to share some of my childhood misery and let him know we had something in common—but no. When he was finished, he jumped to his feet and said, "Gotta get goin'!"

171

I recall one afternoon in particular when the two of us were in his office sitting at his coffee table discussing some project or other, when suddenly a sadness came over him and he got up and moved over to stare out the window. Finally he said, "You know, Bill, I want this Disney thing to go on long after I'm gone. And I'm counting on guys like you to keep it going." "Oh, come on Walt," I scoffed, "you'll outlive every one of us." "No, no, I'm serious, Bill," he said in a hoarse whisper. "I want this thing to keep going." As it turned out, Walt *was* gone a few years after that, and I wasn't around either to keep the "Disney thing going."

After completing the story boards on *The Sword in the Stone* and getting all the voices recorded and ready for animation, I talked Walt into getting the rights to Rudyard Kipling's *Jungle Book*. "A great chance to develop some good animal characters" was my pitch, and he agreed.

I read and reread the Kipling stories until they were well in my mind, then I spent a couple of months writing a script. My secret plan was to work on one more feature picture, something I could enjoy, and then make my getaway, and *Jungle Book* was it.

By that time I had five books in print. After *Huge Harold* there was *Smokey,* about the little switch engine, then *The Pinkish, Purplish, Bluish Egg* and *Ella,* about the spoiled circus elephant. Walt knew I was writing and illustrating books on the side, so I gave *Jungle Book* my best effort in case he should suspect I was putting more thought into my books and neglecting his films.

With such a wealth of characters to develop, sketching the boards was a picnic. There was Mowgli, the fearless waif of a jungle boy, Bagheera, a serious-minded panther, and Baloo, the big playful buffoon of a bear.

There was Kaa, the sneaky, sly python, and Hathi, the bull elephant who didn't trust the man cub or any of his kind.

There were a number of villainous characters in the story, but the scheming, powerful Bengal tiger, Shere Khan, was by far the most threatening. He was obsessed with doing in the man cub.

When I had six or seven boards worked out, I presented that first phase of the story to Walt and the guys. Everyone was excited about the animation possibilities, and Walt was so pleased he came over to shake my hand. He also liked my idea for the song "Bear Necessities," something for Baloo the bear to sing—so I was off and running.

But when the time came to select voices for the characters the picnic was over. The voice I recorded for the leopard annoyed Walt. "That sounds like New York, a Brooklyn accent. That wouldn't fit into this Kipling thing." "He's a good actor," I said. "Why don't I try him again and see if he can get rid of the accent?"

When we met for another story conference, I put the new and improved panther voice on the record player, and as he listened, Walt was glowering at me. "Not one bit better," he grumbled. "Still Brooklyn!" "Okay," I said, "let's forget it. That took only half an hour on the sound stage. I'll find another voice. No problem."

There was a long silence while Walt kept glowering at me. Finally he said, "Can you animate the picture?"

In an attempt at nonchalance I replied, "Why not? I made an animation test while I was working on *Pinocchio* just for the fun of it and it turned out surprisingly good." "What was it," Walt snapped, "the bouncing ball?" The bouncing ball test was the very simplest exercise for beginners, so of course Walt was being sarcastic. "No bouncing ball," I replied. "In fact it was quite complicated. It was an octopus in a panic scrambling over the wreckage of a sunken ship with all eight legs flying in all directions." Walt had no answer for that, and the conference ended with another long silence.

Walt was still fuming as he left his chair and headed for the door. Just before he made his exit he turned to us and said, "If you want to see some *real* entertainment, then see *Mary Poppins!*" And that was the last time I ever saw Walt.

That conference happened to land on January 29, my birthday, and it was after five o'clock when the meeting ended, so it was dark outside. And as I headed for the parking lot, the guys kept their distance. It was the old silent treatment again.

180

That evening, Walt's anger couldn't have been any greater than mine, and as I drove home I was wondering if he intended to kick me downstairs again. Oh no, not this time, I said to myself, because I've got a present for you. Happy Birthday! I'm not ever going back there!!!

When I told Margaret of my birthday present she was not the least bit surprised. She was aware that keeping Walt happy and doing the books on the side was walking a tightrope and after twenty-seven years it was time for a new beginning.

The day after I left the studio I was deeply depressed and kept busy illustrating my sixth book, *Randy's Dandy Lions,* a story about five timid circus lions too jittery to perform their tricks.

One illustration shows the lions cowering in terror as the tyrant of a lion tamer intimidates them by cracking his long, snaky whip in their faces. On the next page, the lions rebel and explode into a fit of thunderous roaring. I wondered if I would have felt better if I had roared back at Walt before I left his studio. As it turned out I'm glad I didn't.

One morning, a little more than a year after I left the studio, when I went out to the driveway to pick up the newspaper, I was dumbfounded at seeing Walt's picture on the front page with the headline "WALT DISNEY, WIZARD OF CARTOON FILMS, DIES." Walt Disney dead?! That didn't seem possible! But there it was in large black print to prove it. That warning cough of Walt's should have been more of a warning to him, for his heavy smoking proved to be his undoing. He died of lung cancer, just like so many heavy smokers.

It would take a long time for me to realize that Walt Disney was gone from this world. As I continued to write and illustrate books in my studio over our garage, I often caught myself wondering what Walt would think of them. I had to get used to the idea that the editor's opinion back in Boston was the one that counted. But first of all I had to please myself, enjoy the work, and write stories about things I liked to draw.

After *Randy's Dandy Lions* I dreamed up *Chester the Worldly Pig,* which included the Indiana farm country, a circus train, and the big top circus of my boyhood years. There is a theory that anything an author writes has some autobiographical aspects to it, and if this is true, then *Chester* is the one book of mine that reflects my past more than any others.

Chester's unhappy beginning in the pigpen compares to my poor beginning in Indianapolis. His accomplishment of balancing on his snout on a fence post to attract the attention of the people on the circus train passing by the farm could be my temporary success as a painter. When Chester escapes the pigpen and runs off down the railroad to join the circus, that is my trip out west to Walt Disney's big top.

When Chester's balancing act gets very little attention, that
is my discouraging start in the Annex. And when the bewildered
pig is put in the big cage with the tigers, that could be my first
years in the story department, where I was squelched by the
fiercely competitive story men and realized my chances of success
were slim and it was more a matter of survival.

Roscoe the clown is Walt Disney, the master showman, who dresses Chester in baby clothes and wheels him around the big top in a baby buggy. Even though I am excited about being part of Walt's act and I am getting a million laughs, my awkward position becomes unbearable and I leave the Disney big top in a huff.

Once he is free of the circus, Chester heads out into the country, where he ends up on a farm in a pigpen. Chester eats his fill every day until he grows into a huge blimp of a pig and the large spots on his side can easily be recognized as maps of all the continents of the world, down to the last detail. A carnival man passing by discovers the unusual spots on the pig and he buys Chester, then puts him in his show as the main attraction, the One and Only Worldly Pig!!

When Chester becomes the center of attention in the big tent show, that could be the recognition I have received for my books, which have been printed in many languages and read by kids all over the world.

Those markings were on the pig from the very beginning just as my ambition to illustrate books was always there. But I never considered writing them, so I had grown far beyond my expectations.